P9-DWT-447

Contents

Part 2
The Deity of Jesus

Part 3
The Deity and Humanity of Jesus

Ken Voges
with Mike Kampainen, Th.D.

UNDERSTANDING
JESUS

A Personality Profile

MOODY PRESS
CHICAGO

ISBN: 0-8024-9083-2

1 2 3 4 5 6 Printing/VP/Year 96 95 94 93 92

Printed in the United States of America

To the Father
for giving us
His Son

Ken Voges (B.S., Texas Lutheran College) is president of In His Grace, Inc., which provides believers and the church with behavioral tools and training. He is the author of the Biblical Personal Profile, an assessment tool that measures behavioral style and relates it to a positive biblical profile. He and Dr. Ron Braund are the authors of the popular book and workbook, *Understanding How Others Misunderstand You*. Serving as field manager for PERFORMAX, Mr. Voges conducts training sessions for the Biblical Personal Profile.

Ken Voges and his wife, Linda, are active in the Spring Branch Community Church in Houston, where he teaches an adult Sunday school class and is chairman of the elder board. They have two children, Randy and Christy.

Mike Kempainen (A.B., Trinity College; Th.M., Th.D., Dallas Theological Seminary) is senior pastor at South Garland Bible Church in Garland, Texas. He and Ken Voges worked together on the PERFORMAX *Biblical Behavioral Series*. He and his wife, Chrysann, have two daughters.

Acknowledgments

I would like to express my gratitude to the people who made special contributions in helping make this book possible:

Dr. Mike Kempainen for his special insights into the Scriptures.

Rich Meiss, Sherry Davis, and Russell Ware for reading and editing the first manuscript.

Jay Conder and Larry Moyer for providing critical insights in presenting the gospel.

Walt Clayton, J. V. Thomas, and Dr. Jimmy McLeod for their prayer support.

The Moody Press family for their encouragement to complete the project.

Linda Voges for loving me when I was unlovable.

Introduction

The Personal Profile of Jesus

Each time I have taught a class or seminar on behavioral styles of biblical characters, invariably someone asks the question, "What was the profile of Jesus?" It is a question that needs to be addressed. Gary Smalley and John Trent believe that He had the strength of all four basic personalities held in balance.[1] That is a good starting point, but what this study will attempt to do is critically look at the three graphs of the DiSC behavioral model[2] and determine whether their premise is true. I believe that it is.

For background, DiSC is a behavior model developed by William Marston in the early 1900s and centers on four basic styles: "D" signifies Dominance, "i" signifies Influencing/Interacting, "S" signifies Steadiness, and "C" signifies Compliance/Cautious.

The Dominance/Dominant style desires to control the environment, whereas the Influencer/Interacting focuses on other people and having fun. The Steadiness style values loyalty and cooperating with others, whereas the Compliance/Cautious style is compelled to do things the "right" way. This particular model has been well researched and tested for validity. It is considered one of the best human resource tools in the industry today.

Smalley and Trent's four-behavior model substitutes animals for DiSC: "D"—Lion, "i"—Otter, "S"—Golden Retriever, and "C"—Beaver. What is important to understand is that no style is better than another in either model. Each style has its own set of strengths that, when left unchecked, can produce an imbalance. Potential strengths can become weaknesses. Only when all the styles function in concert can balance and order occur.

It may appear to some as bordering on blasphemy to speak of Jesus Christ as having a behavioral style or "temperament." However, one of the main doctrines of orthodox, evangelical Christianity is the understanding of the true humanity of the Lord Jesus Christ. Not only was He undiminished Deity in nature but at the same time full humanity, *but without the sin nature.* As theologian John F. Walvoord states, "It is necessary to view Him as having a complete human nature including body, soul and spirit."[3] If this doctrine is correct, and Jesus was who He said He was, the evidence found in Scripture should show His personal profile with human behavior traits, *but always modeling balance and order.*

In theory, "the DiSC research evidence supports the conclusion that the most effective people are those who know themselves, know the demand of the situation, and adapt strategies to meet those needs."[4] Although that is suggested as the ideal, no one is able to do it on a consistent basis. All of the profiles of the DiSC model have imbalanced core styles that are prone to get out of control. As I associated biblical characters with specific patterns, the behavior of Paul, Rebekah, Abraham, Mary, and others confirmed this position. But what about Jesus' style? Does He fit into one specific pattern, or does He respond according to the need of the situation with varying styles, as the ideal would suggest? That is the question that will be studied in this booklet.

How can one effectively research the behavior of Jesus and associate it with the DiSC styles? To do this requires a basic understanding of the DiSC model of behavior. The DiSC model is based on *trait theory*. "It classifies people according to the degree to which they can be characterized in terms of a number of traits. According to trait theory, one can describe a personality by its position on a number of scales, each of which represents a trait."[5] The intensity index of the *Biblical Personal Profile* lists a series of twenty-eight traits on four scales from high intensity to low intensity. Below are examples of these trait words:[6]

High D traits	Low D traits
direct	unassuming
domineering	mild
risk-taker	modest

High I traits	Low I traits
persuasive	controlled
sociable	retiring
confident	aloof

High S traits	Low S traits
patient	mobile
loyal	spontaneous
team person	active

High C traits	Low C traits
accurate	his "own person"
restrained	firm
high standards	defiant

By using this paradigm, or template, we will attempt to associate Jesus' behavior with the eight trait styles (High D, I, S, C; Low D, I, S, C). If our preliminary thesis is correct, Christ's behavior will not fit into one specific pattern, as is normally the case for individuals, but will fill the entire chart. To be more specific, we will be looking for situations in which Jesus exemplifies the entire behavioral range of the styles: from the High D, where He is totally controlling and dominating in confronting specific individuals, to the Low D, where He is a committed, submissive team player; from the High I, where He reaches out to people, to the Low I, where He chooses to be alone; from the High S, where He is patient with others' failures, to the Low S, where He is spontaneous and aggressive in confronting issues; from the High C, where He is diplomatic in accurately communicating Scripture, to the Low C, where He is defiant toward and rebellious against authority figures who try to impose traditions on Him.

With the use of the graphs in *The Biblical Personal Profile* we can research the Lord's style even further. As previously mentioned, the *Biblical Personal Profile* measures three specific behavioral responses on three different graphs. Graph I measures behavior in a given situation, Graph II measures instinctive response under pressure, and Graph III is a summary graph of the first two. We can determine what Jesus was like in a given situation, as for example what He was like when He was with God the Father, or with the Pharisees, or with with common sinners, or even with demons (Graph I). We can also determine what His core behavior was like, or how He handled Himself under pressure (Graph II). Finally, we can combine Graphs I and II into a summary graph (Graph III) to determine who He was.

If Jesus is the Son of God, the challenge will be for the DiSC model to show that His profile includes all

the positive elements of all of the profiles. In addition, His behavior would
have to appear perfect, without im-
balances, in complete control, and in-
stantly able to take on whatever style
is necessary to meet the need of the
situation. Let us begin our study.

PART 1
THE HUMANITY OF JESUS

Graph I:
"Response to Specific Situations"

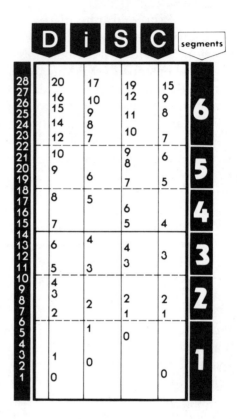

segments	D	i	S	C
6	20 16 15 14 12	17 10 9 8 7	19 12 11 10	15 9 8 7
5	10 9	6	9 8 7	6 5
4	8 7	5	6 5	4
3	6 5	4 3	4 3	3
2	4 3 2	2	2 1	2 1
1	1 0	1 0	0	0

SOURCE: Ken Voges, *Biblical Personal Profiles* (Minneapolis: Performax Systems International, 1985), p. 5. Prepared in association with In His Grace, Inc. (Houston Texas). A product of the Carlson Learning Company. Used by permission of the Carlson Learning Company.

Graph I measures behavior that is perceived to be best suited for a given situation. It is the more dynamic of the three graphs in that it is most subject to change. Graph I's function is to identify a person's response when considering the circumstantial demands of the focused environment; it describes the behavior an individual chooses to project in order to insure the most positive results. It does not necessarily describe who the person really is. In applying Graph I to Jesus, we will look at case studies involving people caught up in highly emotional situations demanding a spontaneous but appropriate response. Special focus will be on the behavior of Jesus as He handled each person's needs within the complexity of that person's circumstances. If Jesus is God, the overwhelming evidence should show that His projected behavior in specific situations not only varied but was perfectly correct to meet the need. In addition, it should be evident from the outcome of the events that the environment Jesus created gave each individual the best chance go grow and mature.

Jesus as a High D

High D traits are characteristic of an individual who imposes powerful control over the environment and the people with whom he comes in contact.

> **Word pictures:** Dominant, demanding, forceful, powerful, authoritative, in control of the environment, intimidating

> **What it produces in others:** Fear and respect, knowing what the High D can do; a personal feeling of weakness in face-to-face encounters; terror, knowing the atmosphere and environment will be confrontational and demanding

It is difficult to think of Jesus as projecting this type of behavior, but when He came in contact with demons, He did just that. Mark 1:21-28 gives a compact example.

Jesus entered the synagogue and began to instruct the people. They "were astonished at His teaching, for He taught them as one having authority, and not as the scribes" (v. 22), that is, the professionally trained scholars. He did not refer to the authority of others but instead gave a more personal interpretation of the Scriptures.

A man in the synagogue who had an unclean spirit interrupted the meeting. "And he cried out saying, 'Let us alone! What have we to do with You, Jesus of Nazareth? Did You come to destroy us? I know who You are—the Holy One of God!'" (v. 24). It is obvious that the demons recognized who Jesus was and who He represented— their Creator, having total authority to judge them.

Jesus responded by saying sternly, "Be quiet, and come out of him!" (v. 25). His tone was demanding, direct, and to the point. The demon shook the man violently and came out of him with a shriek. The people were amazed and profoundly impressed: "What is this? . . . For with authority

He commands even the unclean spirits, and they obey Him" (v. 27).

Conclusion: When Jesus came in contact with demons, He consistently reflected the traits of a High D—total control and authority. Although they had impressive powers, the demons never challenged Him. Instead, they were terrified in His presence. "Powerful and fearful as they are, demons are no match for the Savior, their creator and judge."[7]

Jesus as a Low D

Whereas the High D has a desire to be in control and operate independently, the Low D prefers to be part of a harmonious team. In addition, the Low D tends to project a nonconfrontational spirit, the opposite of the High D.

Word pictures: Peaceful, mild, quiet, unassuming, low-key, soft-spoken, modest, kind

What it produces in others: An overwhelming sense of kindness and unconditional acceptance no matter what you have done; the sense of an environment free of any threat; a feeling of always being able to approach him, knowing that he will never reject you

Jesus tended to project this type of behavior with individuals who were society's rejects. He had several conversations with adulterous women, and one is particularly noteworthy, the encounter found in John 8:10-11. This particular woman was allegedly caught in the act and was condemned to death by the local leaders. Jesus skillfully defused the situation, dismissed her accusers, and turned his focus toward her. Observe what He said.

"When Jesus had raised Himself up and saw no one but the woman, He said to her, 'Woman, where are those accusers of yours? Has no one condemned you?' She said, 'No one, Lord.' And Jesus said to her, 'Neither do I condemn you; go and sin no more'" (vv. 10-11).

The following is a breakdown of the message He communicated to this woman, who a moment before was facing death by stoning:

1. His address was one of respect for her as a person.
2. He did not judge her or declare her innocent.
3. He was interested in forgiving, not condemning, her; He

encouraged her to improve her quality of life and left no doubt He accepted her for who she was.

Conclusion: When Jesus related to repentant sinners, He consistently reflected the traits of a Low D. He had a tendency to be kind toward and understanding of people whom the religious community rejected as worthless outcasts. Though He did not condone their sins, He did accept them as persons—assuring and exhorting them, and being their resource for forgiveness through His relationship with the Father.

Jesus as a High I

High I's are characterized by a desire for involvement with people. Typically they are excellent communicators, using picturesque verbal imagery to express their ideas and feelings.

> **Word pictures:** Interactive, enjoys socializing with others, a master of influencing others with words of assurance and hope, has the ability to sense the needs of others and set in motion the positive energy and inputs to meet those needs

> **What it produces in others:** Reassurance, accepting environments, sense of encouragement and hope in times of despair; a feeling of being shepherded by a person who cares

The Humanity of Jesus

Jesus verbally projected His High I skills in His use of parables (stories related to common experiences but with moral or spiritual meaning). Jesus used this method of teaching in every aspect of His public ministry. More than thirty parables are recorded in the gospels.

Jesus also took the time to reach out to people whenever needs were expressed. Mark 6:34-44 records one of those examples. After hearing about the beheading of John the Baptist, Jesus desired to be alone; however, the people followed Him. When He saw the great multitude, Jesus "was moved with compassion for them, because they were like sheep not having a shepherd. So He began to teach them many things" (v. 34).

As evening was approaching, His disciples came to Him and said, "Send them away . . . for they have nothing to eat" (v. 36). Rather than do that, Jesus sat the people down in groups of fifty and one hundred and performed yet another one of His miracles—He fed five thousand people with five loaves of bread and two fish. It was a marvelous time of fellowship, a wonderful picnic, and a great conclusion to a special day of enlightenment filled with positive surprises and fun.

Conclusion: When Jesus related to the needs of people, He consistently reflected the traits of a High I. He communicated through parables (word pictures) and consistently projected a shepherd's heart in offering hope to the multitudes of people, who were living in a time of misery and despair.

Jesus as a Low I

Whereas the High I prefers to work with people, the Low I is very comfortable working alone. In addition, a Low I is skilled in focusing on the facts of issues, whereas the High I is influenced by social pressure.

> **Word pictures:** Under stress, withdraws to be alone; when alone, has a tendency to spend the time in reassessing objectives, goals, and direction; is the master of his emotions; is able to back off from the emotions of the moment and to keep sight of his goals and objectives

> **What it produces in others:** The sense of being able to count on him to be objective and in control of his emotions when everyone else isn't; assurance that

here is a model of consistency;
confidence that his decisions are
well thought-out and based on
facts and solid principles

Following the miracle of the
feeding of the five thousand, the people, with the support of the disciples,
decided to make Jesus their king (John
6:14-15). They reasoned that He would
be able to meet their physical needs
continually and free them from the
oppression of the Romans.

Jesus understood their motives
and quickly dispatched the disciples
into a boat and dismissed the people
(v. 15; see also Matthew 14:22). He
discerned that this mob action left
unchecked would only serve to thwart
His true mission. What was needed
was to reassess the situation in pri-
vate. When everyone was gone, He,
too, departed to the mountain to pray
and be alone with the Father (Matthew 14:23).

The following are the elements of
the environment He created in dis-
missing the people:

1. Allowed for a cooling down of
   the emotional high experi-
   enced by the people, the disci-

ples, and Jesus (for the record, the positive affirmation of the crowd would fulfill a High I's greatest fantasy yet would get him into serious trouble)

2. Allowed Himself to commune alone with the Father to formulate a better plan of action and communicate clearly who He was and the purpose of His mission (Matthew 14:23-33; 16:13-21)

Conclusion: When Jesus had to respond to issues involving His mission on earth, He was consistently dependent on the Father rather than being influenced by people. He continually spent time alone with the Father to insure that they were together on a plan of action. Behaviorally, this best reflects the traits of a Low I.

Jesus as a High S

The High S is characteristic of an individual possessing incredible patience and constancy. Even in adversity, the High S has the tendency to be extremely loyal to the members of his team.

> **Word pictures:** Steady, patient, loyal, committed to creating harmony, good at follow-through, yet willing to make allowance for mistakes

> **What it produces in others:** Harmony, the assurance that here is someone you can count to be your friend when things are bad, the sense of security in knowing you can make a mistake but won't be rejected

Following the singing of a hymn, Jesus gave the disciples insight into what was about to happen: that night He would be arrested and they would be scattered. He also assured the disciples that He would meet them again in Galilee (Mark 14:26-28).

Peter attempted to convince Jesus that He was wrong and that he was willing to die for Him. Jesus patiently told him that not only would the disciples scatter, but that he, Peter, would deny Him three times. Peter disagreed so vehemently with Jesus that all the disciples felt compelled to say likewise with Peter, "If I have to die with You, I will not deny You!" (vv. 29-31). Jesus listened patiently and reaffirmed what would happen. In addition, He told Peter that Satan had asked permission to "sift you as wheat" (Luke 22:31). Following this comment, Christ confirmed that He had personally prayed for Peter, that he would not be broken but would be strengthened through this experience (v. 32; see also vv. 33-34).

As Jesus was being tried before the high priest, Peter remained in the shadows. A servant girl and two others questioned Peter about his association with Jesus. Peter cursed as he denied the Lord a third time. As the cock crowed, the Lord turned and looked at Peter, communicating disappointment but not judgment (Matthew 26:69-75; Mark 14:66-72; Luke 22:54-62). John 21:15-17 records the resolution of the events. Jesus chose to allow Peter to undo his three denials and restored him to a position of leadership in front of his peers. What patience and grace!

Conclusion: When Jesus was dealing with the disciples and, in particular, Peter, He continually projected unbelievable patience. This trait is most common among the High S profiles.

Jesus as a Low S

Whereas a High S desires structure and order, a Low S profile desires variety and change. In addition, a Low S is skilled at creatively adapting to the needs of a situation, whereas the High S will tend to respond to the same situation with a more traditional approach.

> **Word pictures:** Spontaneous, outgoing, unpredictable, good at assessing the needs and resources of the moment and employing them for maximum effect

> **What it produces in others:** A response, energy resource to challenge the status quo, and an openness to change and possibility thinking

Luke 5:1-11 records the events that led Peter, the professional fisherman, to choose to become a follower of Jesus after a seemingly innocuous event in Peter's village. Jesus happened to be there, and a multitude pressed about Him to hear what He had to say about God. Rather than go into the synagogue, Jesus got into one of the boats, which happened to be Simon's, and cast out a short distance so that all could see and hear Him. Then He sat down and began to teach the multitudes from the boat.

When He had stopped speaking, He said casually to Simon Peter, "Launch out into the deep and let down your nets for a catch" (v. 4). Being a Low S also, Peter "answered and said to Him, 'Master, we have toiled all night and caught nothing; nevertheless at Your word I will let down the net.' And when they had done this, they caught a great number of fish"—so great, they called for help (vv. 5-7).

When Simon Peter saw what had happened he was stunned and "fell down at Jesus' knees, saying, 'Depart from me, for I am a sinful man, O Lord'" (v. 8). Jesus responded by saying to Simon, "Do not be afraid. From now on you will catch men" (v. 9).

So when they (James, John, and Peter) brought their boats to land, they left their jobs and began to follow Him.

Conclusion: Jesus began with a familiar reference point that Peter understood, *fishing*, and creatively used it to inspire him to consider a new ministry. His flexible style and spontaneous action fit Peter's need perfectly. In this situation, Jesus' behavior best represents Low S traits.

Jesus as a High C

High C tendencies are character-istic of an individual who is committed to accuracy and quality control. Typically, once a High C takes ownership of a plan of action, compliance is assured down to the smallest detail.

> **Word pictures:** Perfection, accuracy, courtesy, conscientious model of diplomacy and restraint, absolute commitment to an agreed-upon plan down to the last item

> **What it produces in others:** Conviction that the High C is a model of consistency to be measured by commitment to excellence

Matthew 26:37-56 and Luke 22:39-53 record the agony Jesus went through in the garden in anticipation

of His arrest, beatings, trials, cruci-
fixion, and separation from the Father, and the moment of arrest itself.
As He became sorrowful and deeply
distressed, He humbly prayed, "O
My Father, if it is possible, let this
cup pass from Me; nevertheless, not
as I will, but as you will" (Matthew
26:39). Although honestly expressing
His inner feelings, Jesus remained totally committed to the Father's will
and plan.

While He was still praying, Judas
was on his way with soldiers armed
with swords and clubs to arrest Him.
Jesus was very much aware of their
subversive plan and yet courteously
addressed Judas as His friend.

However, Peter's response was to
cut off the ear of a servant of the high
priest. Jesus reacted by touching the
servant's ear and healing him. Then
He rebuked Peter for his act of vio-
lence and commanded him to put his
sword away. As He exercised these
acts of restraint, Jesus told Peter that
He had available to Him more than
twelve legions of angels (as many as
seventy-two thousand angelic war-
riors of the Lord). All He had to do
was ask the Father, and they would

come to His aid immediately—but that was not the plan.

What was agreed upon between the Father and the Son was for the words of the prophets in the Scriptures to be fulfilled. The disciples would all flee, and Jesus would go to the cross alone—and that is what happened.

Conclusion: Facing certain death, Jesus chose to endure the betrayal, arrest, trial, and cross so that the redemption of man would be completed. In human terms, His incredible restraint could best be described as High C.

Jesus as a Low C

Whereas a High C desires procedures and order, a Low C profile prefers a spontaneous approach. In addition, a Low C is skilled in knowing when to challenge the status quo for the purpose of correction.

Word pictures: Is his "own person," is a nonconformist, can be rebellious, defiant, obstinate, and sarcastic toward individuals he perceives to be hypocritical; has a tendency to be a lightning rod for challenging perceived hypocrisy

What it produces in others: Encouragement to challenge "the system," those who are attacked rally to counterattack, and war often ensues

The scribes and Pharisees continually challenged Jesus because, based on their interpretation of the law, He and His disciples flagrantly violated specific parts of it. The scribes and Pharisees felt compelled to bring those errors to His attention. In Matthew 15:1-14, the specific violation of the disciples was neglecting to wash their hands before they ate.

Jesus aggressively countered the accusations of the scribes and Pharisees by asking them why they selectively nullified God's commandments for the sake of their traditions. "For God commanded, saying, 'Honor your father and your mother'; and, 'He who curses father or mother, let him be put to death.' But you say, 'Whoever says to his father or mother, "Whatever profit you might have received from me has been dedicated to the temple"—is released from honoring his father or mother.' Thus you have made the commandment of God of no effect by your tradition" (vv. 4-6). Then Jesus addressed the crowd and publicly called his accusers hypocrites.

His disciples thought that He was coming on a little too strong and tried to reason with Him in an attempt to get Him to tone down His criticism. "Do you know that the Pharisees were offended when they heard this saying?" (v. 12). Jesus replied by stepping up His criticism of the Pharisees, referring to them as "blind leaders of the blind" (v. 14). In Matthew 23 Jesus' criticism of the Pharisees is also particularly strong.

Conclusion: Jesus reserved His greatest criticism for the religious leaders, particularly the Pharisees, the scholars of the Jewish law. His unrelenting attacks best fit the traits of a Low C and/or a High D.

PART 2
THE DEITY OF JESUS

Graph II:
"Response Under Pressure"

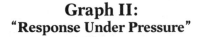

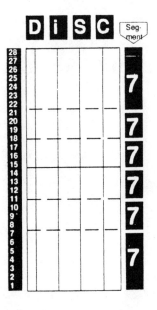

SOURCE: Ken Voges and Ron Braund, *Understanding How Others Misunderstand You Workbook* (Chicago: Moody, 1990), p. 111. Used by permission of Moody Press and In His Grace, Inc.

Graph II defines a person's instinctive response to pressure situations. It is this profile that generally best describes an individual's core behavior. Another way to say it is this: Graph II most often defines the true self, or who a person really is. Whereas all profiles commonly overextend their strengths under stress, Jesus appeared to remain in perfect control. Yet the perception of some individuals was that He had to be dysfunctional. Although the range of behavior He expressed is beyond that of a normal man, another plausible explanation is that Jesus is the Son of God. If Jesus was Deity in a human body, His behavioral traits in Graph II, although identifiable with specific styles, would appear to be supernatural. In addition, His behavior would cover a great range and at the same time be exactly correct and perfect. You be the judge of Jesus' behavior under pressure.

Jesus as a High D Under Pressure

Under pressure High D's tend to become very individualistic and move toward control. It is not uncommon for them to use power words, along with the personal pronouns *I* and *my* to communicate their desires.

A High D's skills and how he influences others: Gifted at finding quick solutions to problems, has the ability to assume leadership in a crisis, is willing to risk challenging outdated, traditional thinking and being the catalyst for developing new systems

How others respond to High D's in pressure situations: Others frequently perceive High D behavior as too direct, egocentric, pushy, and forceful; direct confrontations are common, resulting in painful outcomes; covert actions are frequently used to counter the High D's aggressiveness

Whenever Jesus came into contact with the Pharisees, His behavior can best be described as confrontational. John 8:12-59 is a classic example. The passage is full of control words and conditional clauses introduced by the phrases "unless you," "if you," and "then you will" (depending upon the translation) and is characterized by a dogmatic and authoritative style. In addition, in this one interchange, Jesus uses at least eighty-four personal pronouns, the most common of which are *I*, *My*, and *Me*.

In verses 42 and 47, Jesus challenges the religious leaders by strongly suggesting that they are not of God. Their response is to assert that they are descendants of Abraham and to accuse Him of being possessed by a demon. In verse 58, Jesus uses the words "I say to you, before Abraham was, I AM," not only claiming to have existed before Abraham, but to have eternal existence.

Jesus was taking an incredible risk, claiming to be the Hebrew God of the Old Testament. The Jews understood the significance of His claim, considered it egocentric blasphemy, and took up stones to kill Him.

Conclusion: After it became apparent that they could not overcome His strong High D responses, the religious leaders went to a covert strategy. They were secretly preoccupied with one thought—to kill Him. What they did not realize was that in trying to put Him to death they were unwittingly becoming partners in fulfilling His objective of being the perfect sacrifice.

Jesus as a Low D Under Pressure

Whereas High D's become aggressive under pressure, Low D's become adaptable and submissive. In addition, Low D's will frequently sacrifice personal needs for team goals and not complain.

> **A Low D's skills and how he influences others:** Total commitment to a team concept, unassuming yet thorough in carrying out assignments, incredibly consistent in completing an assigned task

> **How others respond to Low D's in pressure situations:** Others frequently perceive Low D behavior as weak and indicative of an easy prey; whereas their friends tend to take on a rescue mode, their enemies tend to

try to take advantage of them,
knowing they will not retaliate

Matthew 26:31-39 records Jesus' agony in the garden. Facing death, Jesus tried to prepare the disciples for the coming events. The disciples totally misunderstood His message, and Peter led eleven of the twelve to commit themselves to protect Him. With gentle grace, Jesus corrected Peter, predicted his three denials, and called a group prayer meeting. However, the disciples had difficulty staying awake.

Being deeply distressed and sorrowful, Jesus had to face His agony alone with the Father. During one of His prayers, He expressed His concerns regarding taking on the sins of mankind and having to face separation from the Father. However, Jesus concluded His prayer by confirming His commitment to the Father's will and not His own in order to fulfill the prophetic Scriptures and the common goal of the Godhead.

Prior to this prayer, John 17 records what is called the greatest intercession to the Father for the protection of believers. In addition, Jesus confirms the unity of the Godhead with such statements as "That they may all be one, as You, Father, are in Me, and I in You; that they also may be one in Us, and the world may believe that You sent Me" (v. 21). Team unity and commitment are apparent.

Conclusion: With the help of the Romans, the Sanhedrin used its power to crucify Jesus, hoping to put an end to His movement. They did not succeed. The message of the New Testament is that Christ's death on the cross became the ultimate model of submission, as He willingly gave His life so that we can be forgiven and brought into an eternal relationship with the Father.

Jesus as a High I Under Pressure

Under pressure, High I's are capable of verbally attacking others; however, when the environment is without confrontation they tend to reach out to people, including strangers. They are skillful at using small talk to help others feel comfortable before moving to more important topics.

A High I's skills and how he influences others: Gifted people skills, has the ability to communicate a vision through using word pictures that relate best to the audience, a master at spontaneously reaching out to individuals or groups and gaining their trust

How others respond to High I's in pressure situations: With their low expectations of others,

> High I's have a tendency to accept people where they are; close friends, however, are sometimes embarrassed that High I's will talk to anyone they meet—even the outcasts of society

The Jews despised the Samaritans, whom they considered to be lowly half-breeds. Seldom, if ever, would a Jew address them. Yet in John 4:7 Jesus, a Jew, initiates a conversation at Jacob's well with a Samaritan woman. She was shocked that He would talk with her. So were His disciples.

Nevertheless, Jesus openly discussed religious customs, proper forms of worship, her marital history, and the matter of eternal life. Furthermore, it is intriguing how He began the conversation. The woman was there to draw water from the well, so He initiated the conversation by asking for a drink. He skillfully picked up on her reference point of water and spoke of living water. Then He went on to explain how to develop a personal relationship with the Son of God. In this impromptu dialogue are the elements of a solid gospel presentation: assurance of salvation, awareness of a need by confronting sin in one's life, and confirmation that faith in Christ is the means of salvation. It is obvious that Christ's love for all people was greater than His concern for local prejudices and customs.

Conclusion: Although Jesus received criticism from His disciples, the woman went away and gave a positive testimony to her community. Because of her efforts, Jesus was asked to stay in the town an extra two days and present His message to the rest of the villagers. As a result, many believed in Him.

Jesus as a Low I
Under Pressure

Whereas under pressure the High I's will seek to be with people, Low I's under pressure can be aloof and desire to be alone. In addition, Low I's frequently can become introspective.

A Low I's skills and how he influences others: Remains calm and objective in a conflict, is skilled at being able to separate emotions from logical choices, is suspicious of emotional appeals, and is able to focus on solid facts and accurate information

How others respond to Low I's in pressure situations: Others frequently perceive Low I behavior as dispassionate; out of frustration associates will commonly use emotional appeals and confrontation to secure desired feedback, though this seldom works

In Matthew 4, the Spirit led Jesus into the wilderness where He was tested by Satan. Jesus faced Satan on his turf. Jesus used the opportunity to show that even in His weakest condition, He had the resources to withstand the devil at his best. Satan's intermediate goal was to tempt Jesus when He was most vulnerable. His ultimate goal was to destroy God's plan for redeeming mankind by causing the Savior to fall into sin. It was a classic confrontation, with Satan intending evil, as opposed to God, who allowed the testing to reveal righteousness.

Satan's strategy in tempting Jesus was directed at all the basic human needs and senses. In addition, the timing of the temptations came at a point when Jesus would have been most vulnerable—after forty days of fasting. Yet Christ faced and conquered Satan's ploys all alone, and the devil left Him until another opportune time.

Conclusion: Although Satan appealed to His emotions, Jesus never lost control, a response best classified as Low I behavior. When one considers His physical condition, it is obvious that Jesus' response went beyond what is normal even for this style. As the devil tempted Him through deception and misquoting the Bible, Jesus countered by focusing on and responding with the accurate interpretation of the Scripture. The methodical quoting of appropriate biblical verses was His only weapon, a truly remarkable model for us all when we deal with temptation.

Jesus as a High S
Under Pressure

Under pressure, High S's are skilled at directing energy toward building harmony. However, if a confrontational environment persists, they tend to work very deliberately in order to create a calming effect. Their internal need and external goal is to create peace before giving input.

A High S's skills and how he influences others: Gifted at calming excited people; has the ability to create this calming effect by slowing down the pace, using humor, and focusing on facts; verbal tones are generally amiable; nonverbal body language is most often relaxed

How others respond to High S's in pressure situations: If the situation is energy-packed, individuals initially become angered at their inactive response, but, if given the chance, High S skills are often the difference between a disastrous reaction and positive resolution

In John 8:2, Jesus came to the Temple to teach. The people gathered around Him, and He sat down to instruct them. The scribes and the Pharisees apparently decided to create a "no win" situation with the hope of finding some way to bring charges against Him. They had found a woman caught in the act of committing adultery, and they threw her into the center of the crowd Jesus was addressing. Making sure all could hear, they laid out the charge and penalty, making reference to the Mosaic law. Their next response was emphatically directed at Jesus, "You, there! What do you say?"[8] Their intent was to put Jesus in an impossible dilemma.

Jesus' initial response was to write in the sand, His nonverbal action was slow, deliberate, and prolonged. It had the effect, however, of refocusing everyone's attention away from the woman. As this bloodthirsty group persisted in seeking a verbal response, He simply quoted another verse, one requiring those who witnessed the offense and were without sin to cast the first stone. His reply placed the responsibility for any actions squarely on them, not Him. Then He began again to write slowly in the sand. The silence of the moment caused the accusers to think through the consequences of their actions. One by one, starting with the older men, they concluded it was best to drop their rocks and quietly depart until none was left.

Conclusion: Jesus' wisdom was to use a slow, deliberate, silent strategy to defuse the situation. It also saved a life. The behavioral style He exhibited best fits the traits of the High S profile, but goes beyond what one could expect.

Jesus as a Low S Under Pressure

Whereas under pressure a High S prefers a quiet, calm approach to solving conflict, a Low S becomes quite active and aggressive. When facing blatant acts of injustice, a Low S will often take matters into his own hands.

A Low S's skills and how he influences others: Can quickly assess and critically challenge the status quo; knows spontaneously what to do to correct the situation and immediately take action; often, over the long haul, he must pay a high price for those aggressive acts, no matter how noble

How others respond to Low S's in pressure situations: Since Low S behavior demands action, individuals caught in their path tend to respond defensively in pressure situations; sometimes others respond with an even stronger force, and casualties result on both sides

During the time of Jesus, the chief priests allowed the practice of selling animals in the Temple so that pilgrims could offer their sacrifices. They also profited from this marketing enterprise. From Jesus' perspective, that was a desecration of His Father's house and an outrageous insult.

It appears that Jesus drove the money changers out of the Temple on two occasions, once at the beginning of His ministry (John 2:13-17) and once near the end of it (Mark 11:15-17). Both acts appear to be a spontaneous reaction to the noisy marketing activities in His Father's most holy Temple. In the first episode, Jesus made a whip of cords and went after the money changers. In the wild confusion that followed, the animals went scrambling through the aisles, overturning tables and spilling money onto the floor. In the second encounter, the scene and results were the same except that He did not use a whip.

As He was overturning tables, Jesus justified His aggressive actions by quoting the following Scripture: "Is it not written, 'My house shall be called a house of prayer for all nations'? But you have made it a 'den of thieves'" (Mark 11:17). No one dared to challenge Him. When order was restored, He went on healing the blind and the lame.

Conclusion: Jesus' behavior in these passages best fits the High D, Low S profile. Although His actions fulfilled Scripture and cleansed the Temple, it also galvanized the chief priests into action and caused them to speed up the plot to kill Him. Jesus didn't really care, since His plan was to die at their hands.

Jesus as a High C
Under Pressure

Under pressure, High C's tend to be very thorough and respond to questions with precise details. They expect similar responses to their inquiries.

A High C's skills and how he influences others: Gifted at analyzing and researching facts; has incredible recall for details; committed to creating structure and order; skilled at maintaining quality control

How others respond to High C's in pressure situations: Other individuals frequently stand in awe of the High C's ability to communicate facts; however, when High C's make inquiries, others may perceive those in-

quiries as being too detailed
and may choose not to respond

When the people began to recog-
nize Jesus as a respected rabbi, the
scholarly and religious communities
decided to test His knowledge of Scripture. They continually asked Jesus trick
questions, hoping to catch Him in some
error. They wanted to discredit Him
and to develop a charge against Him.
Matthew 22:15-46 records the final
chapter in this type of dialogue.

The Herodians asked Him a question concerning taxes, and He responded, "Render therefore to Caesar the
things that are Caesar's, and to God
the things that are God's" (v. 21). They
marveled at His response and asked
Him no more questions.

Then the Sadducees posed a the-
oretical problem concerning relation-
ships in the afterlife. Jesus responded
by confronting them on their lack of
knowledge of the Scriptures. He care-
fully explained their error in logic and
theology. Then He quoted the proper
Old Testament text and told them
where the emphasis should be.

Now that the Sadducees were si-
lenced, a lawyer of the Pharisees asked
what the greatest commandment was.

Jesus named two: "Love the Lord your God" and "Love your neighbor as yourself" (vv. 37, 39). As they pondered His answer, Jesus turned the tables on the Pharisees with a question of His own regarding the lineage of the Messiah and the fact that David called Him Lord. The Pharisees remained silent.

Conclusion: Jesus' knowledge of Scripture is best reflected in the High C style. Indeed, when people heard Him speak, they came to the conclusion that His understanding was not like that of the scribes because He spoke with personal authority. What He said was either inspired or He had had a hand in the writing of the Scriptures. After this interchange, no one challenged Him.

Jesus as a Low C Under Pressure

Whereas a High C tends to project a cautious and restrained atmosphere under pressure, a Low C becomes arbitrary and blunt. When Low C's or their associates are attacked, they often become obstinate and rebellious.

A Low C's skills and how he influences others: Independent thinker, enjoys challenging assignments, is skilled at leading in situations where he is in total control of implementing the methods of operation

How others respond to Low C's in pressure situations: Since Low C individuals have a tendency to be independent and to demand being their "own person," others who try to bring them under control generally find the process difficult, if not impossible; when a Low C encounters those who want to bring him under control, sparks generally fly

Matthew 12:1-14 pictures Jesus and His disciples walking through grain fields on the Sabbath. Being hungry, they plucked heads of grain and ate them. The Pharisees saw them do that and accused Jesus and His disciples of violating the Pharisees' interpretation of the Sabbath laws. Jesus bluntly questioned their understanding of Scripture and gave them an example that refuted their position. In verse 8, He firmly tells them that the "Son of Man," Jesus, has been given the authority to handle the Sabbath law any way He wills. Then He defiantly ended the conversation and walked away.

Stunned, the Pharisees followed Him into the synagogue and came upon a man with a shriveled hand. Trying to recover, they asked Jesus, "Is it lawful to heal on the Sabbath?" (v. 10). The purpose of the question was to find some reason to accuse Him.

Taking up their challenge, Jesus chose to make a point that totally rejected their rigid interpretation of the law. He asked the Pharisees a question concerning the value of man and the importance of reaching out to meet needs as a higher calling than being concerned about rules. As a final act of defiance toward them, He healed the man's arm in *their synagogue as they watched.*

Conclusion: Jesus' behavior in these passages best fits the High D, Low S, and Low C traits. Although uncharacteristic of Jesus, this defiant style was appropriate for the situation and showed incredible courage.

PART 3

THE DEITY
AND
HUMANITY OF JESUS

Graph III:
"Self-Perception"

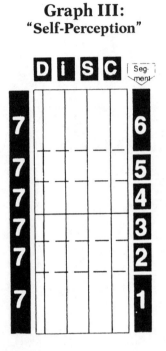

SOURCE: Ken Voges and Ron Braund, *Understanding How Others Misunderstand You Workbook* (Chicago: Moody, 1990), p. 111. Used by permission of Moody Press and In His Grace, Inc.

In the DiSC system, the third graph provides a description of an individual's self-identity. It is a summary graph that combines the expected behavior of Graph I with the core behavior of Graph II. Based on the evidence recorded in Scripture it appears that Jesus expressed all the human behavior traits listed on all four DiSC scales. What makes Jesus unique is that whatever style He expressed, it was the right one for the specific situation. Behaviorally, the evidence strongly suggests He had to be God. No other conclusion can be rationally supported, based on the range of His behavioral responses.

The individuals who spent the most time with Him came to a similar conclusion. His best friend, John, says, "And truly Jesus did many other signs in the presence of His disciples, which are not written in this book; but these are written that you may believe that Jesus is the Christ, the Son of God, and that believing you may have life in His name" (John 20:30-31).

Although some were confused about who He was, when Jesus asked the disciples what their perceptions were, Peter, the leader of the disciples, responded, "You are the Christ, the Son of the living God" (Matthew 16:16).

God the Father spoke three times in the gospels. Twice He directly confirmed that Jesus was indeed His Son. The first occasion was at Jesus' baptism (Mark 1:11); the second was at Christ's transfiguration (Matthew 17:5).

When the demons encountered Jesus, they always referred to Him as Deity. On one occasion the demons within two possessed men called Him "Jesus, You Son of God" and humbly begged Him not to torment them (Matthew 8:27).

However, the problem still exists: how can the behavior of man be associated with God? The apostle Paul deals with the dual nature of Jesus' humanity and divinity in Philippians 2:5-11. Paul says that Jesus did not demand to remain in the "form" of God but chose to limit His outward expression of His true inward deity. His purpose was to fulfill His mission among mankind, and He took on the outward expression of mere mortal man (human behavior of Graph I). It was in this form that He humbled Himself to die on the cross. However, though the humanity of Jesus was real and true (complete humanity without sin), He remained, at the same time, undiminished Deity (Graph II). When the two graphs are put together to complete Graph III, one has a model of Jesus as 100 percent man and 100 percent God—which fits the theology of the New Testament in its description of the character of Jesus Christ, the Son of Man.[9]

What should this all mean to you?

By viewing the behavior of a person over an extended period of time, one is able to gain insight into that person's character. As we have looked at the behavior of Jesus during the three and one-half years of His public ministry, we have observed something that can be said of no other person in history. Jesus was able both to be flexible in the temperament He projected and to always select the behavioral style that was exactly right for the situation. The only way to understand this to believe what the disciples proclaimed—that He is the Son of God who came to earth to die for the sins of mankind.

John tells us that by receiving Him (as personal Savior) we become God's children (John 1:12). The apostle Paul says that we do this by faith (believing that His death on the cross is sufficient for our forgiveness) and not by our own good works or righteousness (Ephesians 2:8-9). Paul also tells us that every human being is sinful and needs the forgiveness that Jesus Christ offers freely to everyone who will believe and receive it (Romans 3:10, 23; 6:23).

Just as the personality of Jesus Christ is supernatural, so is the forgiveness that He offers to us. It takes the supernatural change that comes through faith in Christ to transform our shortcomings in personality. We can become more flexible and useful to God and can strengthen the limitations of our own temperaments only in Jesus Christ. But even more important, we can be forgiven of the sin in our lives and have the assurance of eternity with God by believing in and accepting the One who demonstrated by His behavior that He is truly the eternal Son of God.

This belief in Him brings with it an eternal relationship with God (John 3:16). God allows you the free will to decide for yourself whether to believe the gospel of the New Testament and receive the benefits of salvation or to reject the gospel and suffer the consequences of that rejection (1 John 5:12). The choice is yours to make.

Notes

1. Gary Smalley and John Trent, *The Two Sides of Love* (Pomona, Calif.: Focus on the Family, 1970).

2. Ken Voges, *Biblical Personal Profile* (Minneapolis: Carlson Learning Company, 1984), p. 5.

3. John F. Walvoord, *Jesus Christ Our Lord* (Chicago: Moody, 1967, p. 111.

4. *The Personal Profile System* (Minneapolis: Performax Systems International; Carlson Learning Company, 1977; rev. 1986), p. 1.

5. William Marston, *Emotions of Normal People* (Minneapolis: Persona, 1977), p. xxiii.

6. The Complete DiSC intensity index with all 112 trait words can be found in the workbook *Understanding How Others Misunderstand You*, by Ken Voges and Ron Braund (Chicago: Moody, 1991), p. 24.

7. C. Fred Dickason, *Demon Possession and the Christian* (Chicago: Moody, 1987), p. 31.

8. Frank E. Gaebelein, ed., *The Expositor's Bible Commentary*, vol. 9 (Grand Rapids: Zondervan, 1981), p. 90.

9. A more complete picture of how these graphs look can be found in the workbook *Understanding How Others Misunderstand You*, Appendix C, pp. 109-12.

Jesus Claimed

(JOHN 8:58)

Two

His claims were FALSE

Two Alternatives

He knew His claims were FALSE	He did not know His claims were FALSE
He made a deliberate misrepresentation	He was sincerely deluded
He was a LIAR	He was a LUNATIC
(The opinion of the Pharisees)	(The opinion of those in His hometown)

to Be God

Alternatives ──────┐
                   │
                   │
His claims were TRUE
                   │
        HE IS LORD
                   │
   ┌── Two Alternatives ──┐
   │   │
   │   │
You can   You can
ACCEPT   REJECT
(John 3:16)